The Four Seasons

Written and illustrated by
Monique A. Nimely

To order additional copies of this book, contact:
Xlibris
1-888-795-4274
www.Xlibris.com
Orders@Xlibris.com

The Four Seasons

Written and illustrated by

Monique A. Nimely

Contents

Spring

Spring

A time when it's not too hot and not too cold.

If you ask me, I would think this season is quite bold!

This is the time that's right before summer,

And trust me it will not be a bummer.

Summer

Summer

We can all finally take a break from school.

My favorite part is when we go to the pool.

If you're lucky, there's no homework to do!

What's your favorite part of summer?

Fall

Fall

There are so many things to do in this season.

I can't even start with a reason.

The leaves are pretty, and the weather is chilly.

Winter is almost here, so get ready!

Winter

Winter

It's snowing and Christmas is around the corner.

We can have snowball fights across the border.

We get warm by drinking hot cocoa,

While someone else might be drinking an ice mocha!

My favorite season is spring! What's your favorite season? ☺

About The Author

Monique was born on May 30th 2006 and she is in the fifth grade. She has always had the talent for visual arts which she improved by watching TV, copying the styles of the art and mixing them up into her own new design. As a toddler in preschool, she started off by drawing a purple bumpy line and calling it a cat. Everyone said it was good and she liked that feeling so she kept practicing and practicing and soon she could draw ponies and people and anime.

Printed in the United States
By Bookmasters